"I'm 55 and I Hate My Job!"

Stories and Solutions from an Executive Coach

Scott Robinson

Cover design by Sara Millsap www.saramillsap.com

Author photo by Portrait Innovations, Inc.

Interior book design by Debbie Manning www.debmanning.com

Book production by Dianne Morr www.diannemorr.com

ISBN 978-0-692-02725-7

To my family—Deb, Paige and Taylor,
who have supported me through my personal transition

Table of Contents

Preface

This book began as a way to keep track of the many opportunities I have encountered in the process of coaching executives. While this book certainly does not cover every situation, I have tried to include some of the common challenges executives face and how my clients and I have resolved them. I believe that others might learn from these stories and be able to apply some of the principles to their own situations. It is my desire to assist as many executives as possible with these stories.

All of the names in this book have been changed as well as any company or industry identities. Thanks to everyone whose examples are included in hopes that others will learn through their experience.

It has been my experience that while everyone's situation is different, there are many similarities. By recounting our effort to assist in performance enhancement, succession planning, and in some cases intervention, we hope to coach, teach, and support executives in their growth as leaders.

Chapter **1**

Clarity

Know Your Destination Before You Chart the Course

I f you are 55 and you hate your job, you know you want something to change. You may feel trapped, bored, or overwhelmed, and you dread spending even one more day, let alone another 10, 20, or 30 years, continuing in the same role.

In order to figure out what really needs to happen in your life, you need to get a clear vision of who you are and what you want. That's the step you have to take before you can figure out where you are going and how you can get there.

What you need can be summed up in one word: *clarity*.

My Story

I was fortunate to have a father who gave me a gift that few teenagers ever receive—the gift of clarity. When I was 13 years old, he asked me, "Scott, when you think about your life as an adult, what do you see? Imagine that you can have anything in the world. What does your life look like?"

I was young, but those questions didn't take me by surprise. I already had some pretty vivid dreams of what my future looked like.

Growing up in a small town in Illinois, I knew I wanted to live in a bigger place with more going on. "I want to be living in a nice suburb of Chicago," I told him. "I see myself in a beautiful, comfortable house and I'm married to a beautiful woman. We'll have two kids, a boy and a girl." We were getting pretty detailed here.

Even at 13, I was already a car guy. "I'll be driving a luxury car. In fact I might want more than one, maybe a sports car just for fun.

"I want a cabin in the country somewhere near some water—a river or a lake. And I'll need a boat because I will want to be out on the water and maybe do some fishing.

"I want my own helicopter so I can fly back and forth between the house and the cabin." I think my dad may have had to work to keep from chuckling, but he honored my dreams as completely possible.

"And I want to have my own business and be my own boss."

Besides having a father who took my dreams seriously, I had a mother who let me know I had the ability to do anything I wanted. She was a very bright lady and held the position of vice president and manager of a bank. (I am sure she could have gone further in her career with the right educational opportunities.) She wanted me to know I didn't have to settle for just a job or for anything less than I was capable of dreaming.

I have been blessed in so many ways that have allowed me to reach all of those goals. In the rest of this book, I will share the details of my journey and what I have learned along the way.

The First Lesson

I was fortunate enough to have parents who helped me to clarify my life dream as a child. You may have had a parent like mine or an advisor or mentor who guided you early in your life. But the fact that you knew who you were and what you wanted then doesn't mean you are still the same person right now.

A classic rite of passage of young adulthood is the identity crisis. You may have figured out who you were at 18 or 19, and this is sometimes the case for doctors or lawyers, but it is usually the rare exception. If you feel stuck in your job right now and dread going to work in the morning, it's time to ask some questions and discover who you are now. You have grown and changed in many ways since that identity crisis in your teens.

As you start on this quest for clarity it can be very helpful to work with a journal where you can record your thoughts—the questions you want to ponder, the frustrations you are feeling, the wishes and ambitions you have for the future. Don't dismiss this idea as too touchy-feely. Every office supply store carries an assortment of professional-looking journals or notebooks that can become a reliable tool to use as you gain the clarity you need to advance toward your dreams.

Dreams

To begin your journey toward clarity, ask yourself the questions my father asked me. Picture your ideal life and describe it in detail. You may have reached an age at which some people retire. But whether you are employed or retired, you can look forward to another 25 to 30 years to enjoy. How do you want to spend those years? What pursuit do you find fulfilling? Do you want another career more aligned with your passion? Do you want to find a way to give back to the community?

Figure out your priorities. What are your goals, hopes, dreams, or plans in regard to:

- Family

- Autonomy

- Wealth

- Spirituality

- Social Responsibility

- Health

Andrea was a client I coached a few years ago. She served a medium-sized, privately-held company as a very competent controller. When the chief financial officer left for a new job, the company president promoted Andrea to CFO. The C-suite executives were sure she could handle that responsibility.

When her company did not backfill the controller job right away, Andrea found herself acting as both CFO and controller at work. The controller job required that she look at all checks, all decisions by her team, and even monitor all expenses of her peers and their departments.

At home, Andrea and her husband were raising three active children. She also handled all the family finances and took care of all those financial details—checks, expenses, and decisions—for her family, too.

At work, as at home, Andrea had difficulty changing hats and delegating the details of the controller role because there was no one identified to take over. Adding the responsibility for all the high-level, big-picture decisions as the CFO made the workload unbearable.

One day, after a disaster within the company where a storm took out all power and flooded the entire operation, Andrea experienced an acute stress disorder response while on the job, necessitating a medical leave. Andrea's health demanded that she rest and reassess her priorities, responsibilities, and opportunities.

She recognized that the overload of multiple financial responsibilities at work and at home was taking a toll on her health and her family life—two important priorities.

When she returned to her job, we worked together to hone her skills to manage her responsibilities as a CFO and let go of the controller responsibilities. Learn more about how she learned to delegate controller tasks in Chapter 2.

In order to learn best practices for handling CFO responsibilities, I recommended that Andrea join an organization of CFOs. Meeting with others in the same role gave Andrea access to ongoing learning opportunities and a sounding board to talk about issues CFOs face.

How Do Others See Me?

To help you figure out who you are at this point in your life and what path you want to follow, you need a realistic picture of your strengths and weaknesses. One challenge in figuring out your strengths and weaknesses is that it is almost impossible to be objective.

One solution is to ask a trusted friend or colleague to help you. Spend some time with someone who knows you well, other than your spouse—possibly a supportive sibling or a close friend. Ask him or her: "What do you see that I am good at? What strengths do you see in me?" The answers may surprise you.

The next step will probably make you feel a little vulnerable, but ask what you are not good at. You might see yourself as easygoing and able to roll with the punches, but people close to you might tell you that you really want/need to do things your own way.

The answers you receive may shed new light on why you are feeling trapped or stressed in your current job. They may give you a new approach to using your strengths to do your job differently. Or they may inspire you to take a new direction in a whole new field. Proactively asking for a reality check on how you are doing is a smart move if you are unhappy in your job.

Sometimes you may hear that type of feedback without requesting it. If there is conflict in your work relationships, you may be forced to look at how others see you.

A Sales Manager Learns Leadership Skills

Len was a senior sales executive who thought the people on his team should do what he wanted them to do without question. He made it clear that he didn't care if his sales team was happy or unhappy. He was the boss and they had better listen to him because he was the sales expert. *Besides,* he thought, *if you pay them well, that's all that matters. After all, isn't that why they got into sales?*

Two people on the executive team went to the CEO and said, "If you don't do something about this guy, we're either going to kill him or quit because we can't deal with him anymore."

That was when Len and I were introduced. During a 360-degree evaluation with his peers and coworkers, I learned how they perceived his communication style and attitude. Next I asked Len to complete a leadership effectiveness assessment, and a lot of details came to light. He scored very low on empathy and communication but very high on feedback. That combination is the Bermuda Triangle of scores for a manager of a team. Those scores indicated he didn't give good direction and he didn't care what others thought or how they felt, but he would be the first to criticize anyone who fell short of his expectations.

When it came time for Len and me to sit down together, I had to be blunt. "You're not a very well-liked guy here and it's making your job harder," I said. "So, you need to decide if you want to stay at this company, add value, and get cooperation from your team. If you don't make changes, you will eventually get fired."

I used the scores from his assessment coupled with the feedback from his team to invite him to look at his situation. I told him, "You need to figure out what about your current style is not working and what actions will ultimately not only make the company successful but also make you successful."

Len realized that his job and his compensation were worth more than his ego and his attitude, so he decided to alter his behavior. We spent the next six months talking about his communication style, his behavior in meetings, how he delegated work and communicated directions. We also discussed how to give feedback that expressed his feelings appropriately.

The most important change took place when I told Len that he needed to go into the office of at least one or two people every single day to get to know them on a personal level. He visited peers and subordinates and occasionally someone he didn't even know. These visits allowed him to understand people's individual situations and gain higher levels of empathy. He learned to understand a factory worker out on the line making $18 an hour trying to support four children and a wife who's not been healthy. He learned that his job is not just all about proclaiming edicts and delegating and firing. It's about working with real people.

Sometimes you have to work around people's issues to make them successful. The outcome is that Len learned to be a leader and became a much more effective and understanding manager. He became happier at work and his team did, too.

Career Design by You or by the Company

You might wonder how someone like Len finds himself in a job that doesn't fit his personality or aptitude. His situation is not at all uncommon. Len let his company move him along a career path because it was convenient, because they needed somebody, and because they thought he could do that particular job well. Technically he did what needed to be done as the head of sales. It just wasn't a good fit for him personally or socially, and he wasn't happy doing it. Unfortunately, rather than driving his own career and telling the company what he wanted to do, he allowed the company to make those decisions.

Frankly, this kind of situation happens to a lot of people. When you're young you might begin a job, then you are offered an opportunity making more money and you say, "Okay, I'll take that." You do a good job and then another opportunity comes up with a better title, a bigger office, and more money. Then you're offered a company car and then a bonus check and then stock options. Before you know it, you're 40 or 50 years old and you're a vice president.

Still, you haven't been the person to design your career. You've just been moved into those roles because you have performed well. But successfully performing a job doesn't necessarily mean you're happy with what you are doing. I see it in sales all the time. The company takes their best salespersons and ruins them by moving them into management.

I have been coaching a sales executive who says, "I don't even want to be in this job. I was happy selling. Quite frankly, I was making more money when I was selling. Now I've got 18 direct reports, and I'm copied on 2,000 emails going back and forth. I don't really like doing this."

That happened because the company needed him in that role. He was successful in sales, so they felt he would probably be a successful sales manager. He may be a successful sales manager, but that doesn't mean he's enjoying it.

Where Are You Now?

If you hate your job right now, it may be hard to like anything about it. But maybe you remember what you liked about it when you accepted it.

Ask yourself, "What's good about the job I have?" Consider some of the following factors:

- *Job satisfaction.* Possibly the most important factor in making any career decision is job satisfaction. If you feel rewarded because your job makes a contribution to your community or makes the world a better place, many other factors take on less importance.

- *Geography.* Are you working in a location you love?

- *Salary.* Does your income provide for your needs, wants, and long-term goals?

- *Commute.* Does a local or in-home office minimize your time on the highway?

- *Travel / Freedom from travel.* Are you happy with the amount of time you spend away from home?

- *People.* Do your work colleagues feel like friends?

Then review this same list and find the possible drawbacks of your current situation:

- *Job satisfaction.* If the work you are doing is not rewarding in itself, other positives may not make up for that deficiency.

- *Geography.* Are you living in a climate that you hate or at a distance too far from family and friends?

- *Salary.* Do you feel underpaid for your contribution to the company? Are you feeling strapped for money? Or is your salary a golden ball and chain making you feel you can't afford to take any chances?

- *Commute.* Are you driving 90 minutes twice a day between your home and office?

- *Travel.* Are you flying out of town every Monday morning and returning Thursday night? Are you missing important family time?

- *People.* Do you work with toxic people who radiate negativity?

Once you see and consider the pros and cons of your job, it will be a lot easier to decide if you want to find a new job or learn to love the one you have.

Knowing What You Want and What You Don't Want

Having your dream life in view allows you to create a roadmap to get there. Using your journal or working with a career counselor can help you figure out the answers to these questions: Did you have a dream early in your career? Did you reach it? Are you still striving for that same dream?

In addition to knowing what you want, knowing what you *don't* want is important. What is not working in your life? What would have to change in order for you to feel like you are living the life you were meant to live? It is also realistic to consider what just might be impossible for you to have right now.

About 15 years ago, my childhood best friend introduced me to Jimmy John Liautaud, founder of Jimmy John's Gourmet Sandwiches. We have all been great friends ever since, in part because the three of us enjoy outdoor activities such as hunting, fishing, snowmobiling, motorcycling, and flying.

Jimmy John explained how he started his business. He had not been the best student in high school. In fact, he graduated second-to-last in his class, so he didn't plan to go to college. His father thought the structure of the military would be good for him and wanted him to enlist in the Army. But Jimmy John did not want to be a soldier. The two made an agreement that Jimmy John's dad would make a loan to him to finance starting a business. If the business failed, Jimmy John would join the Army.

Although his original plan was to open a hot dog restaurant, Jimmy John realized the loan from his dad wouldn't stretch far enough to cover all the equipment needed to cook hot dogs. That's how he settled on offering gourmet sandwiches. For sandwiches, the only special equipment he needed was a meat slicer and a refrigerator.

Jimmy John's knowledge of what he didn't want—to join the Army—motivated him to build a successful business into a sandwich empire. The Jimmy John's Gourmet Sandwich brand is now a billion dollar industry with more than 1,750 locations across the country and growing.

Where You Want to Be and How You Want to Get There

If you hate your job, there are so many things to clarify. Once you know where you are and where you want to be, you will find out that there are different ways to get there. These are some of the questions you need to ask:

- Do I want a different job or do I want to change the way I do my current job?

- Do I want to find a new job within the same company or go to a new company?

- Do I want to keep my current job while I look for a new job or quit my current job and devote all my time to the search?

Next Steps

Once you have gained clarity on who you are at this point in your life and where you want to be, you will be prepared to look at your options. By reflecting on what you want and what you don't want, you will begin to find more opportunities. You are starting on an exciting journey.

If you have not already reflected on your ultimate life goals and created a detailed description of how you want to end up, it is time to reread the last three pages with a notebook or journal in hand. Write down your answers to the questions that start on page nine.

Chapter 2

Workload

Do You Really Hate It, or Do You Just Need to Do It Better?

With all the workforce reductions and cost savings that have gone on since the economy went south in the last five or six years, a lot of small- to medium-sized companies or young entrepreneurial and growing companies have cut their staffs to the bone. Others are trying to grow and keep their costs down. The result is that a lot of senior managers have become overly involved in the tactical areas of their companies. They are performing what I call "work in the weeds"—a lot of the tactical work—and focusing on the day-to-day. Their time and effort would be better spent managing the strategic directions, implementing strategy and mission, or staying focused on long-term growth.

All the emphasis in these organizations seem to be focused on:

* Short-term goals and objectives

* Short-term stockholder value for the current year

* Profit for the current month or for the current bonus schedule

The word I am constantly hearing from clients is "burnout." Sometimes it may seem that word is overused, but burnout lives right next door to "hate my job." Senior managers are saying they just don't have any time: the day-to-day immediate work is a constant, leaving no time for long-term focus.

I was in a meeting just this morning sitting with nine CEOs, some heading million dollar companies, some heading multi-billion dollar companies. Seven of the nine complained about the same thing. "I just don't have any time." For some, the time crunch plays out in life-balance issues around spending time with family and friends. For others, their lack of time means they are not able to address the larger-scale issues or to grow their businesses strategically.

The tool that I find most effective in addressing my clients' time problems is what I call the *DEAD* strategy. I joke that it works great for people who feel like their organizations are dead or their energy level is dead.

DEAD is an acronym for a system to divide your workload into four distinct categories:

- Delegate
- Eliminate
- Automate
- Do it

I like to look at the work that arises in a particular day or week or month. This tool makes it easy to see what activities are taking up most of your time. Let's say you get all kinds of work coming in regularly. I try to break it out on a weekly basis. I ask presidents or senior leaders to break their workload into four separate and distinct categories or piles.

Give Me a D

The first D stands for **Delegate.** As work comes in, I ask people to carefully make a determination as to whether this is something they can delegate. They need to ask, "Is there someone in my organization I can delegate this to, to take it off my plate so I can think more broadly or strategically?"

That usually brings up two possibilities. One, I can delegate this and get it off my plate, so I need to do that rather than just go ahead and handle it myself. Two, it doesn't really belong on my plate but I don't have anybody I can delegate this to. If there is no one I can delegate to, then either:

- We cut our organization too deeply

- We don't have a strong enough bench

- I need to look at my own delegation skills and my mentality as it relates to letting others handle more responsibilities.

As CEO or the senior leader, do I cause my own problems with time management because I need to improve at delegating? You'd be surprised at how many senior-level people I need to force to delegate or to delegate better. They ultimately do, and they like getting the work done by somebody else who probably is better at it or more knowledgeable than they are.

Delegating not only gets the task off the CEO's plate, it also expands the horizon of subordinates and allows them to enjoy their jobs more. It gives the delegate more access to the larger issues going on within the company.

Do you remember Andrea, the CFO from Chapter 1? Learning to delegate was one of the most important skills she developed that allowed her to let go of day-to-day controller responsibilities. In order to delegate, she needed to look at the whole team to recognize strong

players who needed to be held accountable. She also needed to identify weak players who either needed more training or mentoring, or
who needed to be replaced. With the team strengthened, there were
people who could be trusted with more responsibility.

Give Me an E

The second category is *Eliminate*. How much unnecessary work,
energy, effort, and time am I spending on things that I really don't
even need to be thinking about? It's just noise that I need to block
out. Examples on my desk include taking the time to unsubscribe to
emails that come through and throwing junk mail in the trash. The
bigger picture includes tasks that go on within my company that really
are not necessary any longer. Sometimes we've been doing something
a certain way forever; we continue to do it even though it is not necessary. These things can easily be eliminated.

Give Me an A

The third category is *Automate.* Automation is a concept that is sometimes foreign to CEOs and senior leaders. In this use, the word "automate" doesn't have to mean "computerize" or "mechanize." Any task
or issue that comes up on a regular basis can be automated by creating a process or procedure for handling it. If you find yourself handling
repetitive tasks, it's time to document the steps you take to complete
or resolve them.

In addition, there may be other tasks you handle that could be turned
over to a process that your IT department creates.

Give Me Another D

The fourth category is simply *Do It.* This is what I should be doing. I
can't delegate it, I can't eliminate it, I can't automate it. This is
my responsibility.

Over a period of time, if you sort work items into the *DEAD* categories, note which list grows the fastest. That will tell you if you have a problem in one area. For example, if the *Do It* list is constantly longer than the *Delegate* list, you may not be acting with a senior leader mentality. You may need to get better at your delegation skills. You may need to develop someone on your team to create better bench strength, or you may need to bring someone in from outside so that you can delegate to him or her. That will free you to work on senior-level issues and strategies.

The *Eliminate* list is easy. If that keeps getting longer—that's great. We're not going to worry about that.

If the *Automate* list keeps getting longer, that's great, too. That signals fewer things you need to worry about. The *Eliminate* and *Automate* areas are great ways to keep score on whether you are using your time on the important things. So we want to find more ways to eliminate and automate work.

The two critical areas that I'm looking at are the Ds—*Delegate* and *Do It*. These are the areas where we get control of our time.

The DEAD Strategy in Action

Jay is the president of a company that has about $30 million in revenue. It's a growing company; their goal is to get revenue to $50 million. Over the last six years, they have watched cost containment and have done a great job of that. They've been very profitable, so they have money to spend.

They've been very conservative, their business is on the uptick, and their margins remain attractive. Therefore, the company is highly profitable. We needed to work with Jay to put a strategy in place and have a strategic conversation with his board.

We broke down Jay's work into the four *DEAD* categories and found out that Jay was doing way, way too much tactical work. He was physically and/or mentally performing work that should have been delegated to people at a level below him, and in some cases two levels below him. We kept track of Jay's four lists and we found that his *Do It* list kept getting longer and longer. The other lists were staying the same or were getting smaller, showing that there was an imbalance.

We determined that Jay didn't want to let go of the control of some things that were way below his level of concern. I challenged him and said, "Jay, I notice on your *Do It* list that you were very involved in the branding message." The company was introducing a new product line and they were working on how to position it. He was not just approving what marketing was doing; he was sitting in on low-level marketing meetings with the outsourced group and helping them. He was getting into logo design, the brand message, the colors of the logo, their demographics, and how they were going to bring it to the marketplace. The work was just way down in the trenches, way down in the organization.

Those meetings could have gone fine without him. A representative of marketing could have come to him and said, "This is what we've done, this is our research, this is the proposal, these are some logo ideas that we've come up with, this is the branding strategy we'd like to take." Marketing could do a presentation for him and he would approve it, tweak it, or not approve it. Instead, he spent a lot of time in long meetings over a long period of time.

Looking at his workload, we found that he didn't have a strong enough marketing department, or a marketing department that he trusted. He either needed to get comfortable with delegating to the marketing team or he needed to realize that he wasn't going to have any time.

In Jay's case, he was a young CEO—39 years old. In time, he might have learned to become a higher-level thinker and a higher-level leader than he was at that time. With the help of the *DEAD* strategy, we were able to shorten his learning curve greatly and help accelerate the growth of the company.

Jay needed to tell the board, "We must bring a couple of carefully selected, high-level people into our organization to strengthen the marketing department. This means we may need to terminate two of our senior leaders to upgrade that talent from the outside. Qualified people from the outside are going to cost us more money than we have been paying these two particular leaders who report to me."

Jay and I put together a communication strategy, not only about what he needed to do and how he needed to do it, but also about how important this change would be for the overall long-term strategic growth of the business. Jay also needed to talk about how this could impact their profitability, at least in the short term.

The board needed to know upfront that their returns on investment may be less because it's going to cost them more to do business. However, the long-term gains should be greater because the changes will give Jay more time to spend on more important strategic areas of the business. We developed this strategy when we looked at what he was doing and how he was doing it.

Looking at your workload with *DEAD* in mind, you also should find more tasks going to the Delegate list compared to the *Do It* pile. Or, you may come to another realization.

Once in a while, a senior leader realizes that he has been choosing to do more hands-on work because he really likes doing that better than creating and implementing strategy. An exaggerated example might be the president of Wal-Mart wanting to be a greeter. You can't be everywhere and do everything. You have to trust that the greeters at your store are smiling and shaking hands and welcoming your customers.

Sometimes a client considers the hands-on work he or she is doing and says, "This is really what I like to do." Then we shift gears and get into a completely different discussion starting with, "Well, maybe you shouldn't be a senior leader." If you really like drawing buildings and drawing the infrastructure for a house, or a building, or a railroad, maybe you shouldn't be the president of a construction company. Maybe you should go back to being an architect.

Sometimes, when we look at a senior leader's workload or job fit, we shift the discussion to "Do I really want to be a better leader or do I really want to be a doer?" In the process of determining how to be a better leader, a client could come to the conclusion that she thought she always wanted to run a company or to be vice president of engineering, but she really likes being an engineer. You can't do both. Analyzing your workload and job fit allows you to see where you are spending your time. It's up to you to decide if you want to change your workload by delegating better or whether you might want to rethink your career goals.

Chapter 3

Attitude

Are You Your Own Best Friend or Worst Foe?

Everything can be taken from a man but one thing: the last of human freedoms—to choose one's attitude in any given set of circumstances, to choose one's own way.

Viktor E. Frankl, *Man's Search for Meaning*

My mother-in-law, Bernice Brue, is 87 years old and still very dynamic and active. She is a little over five feet tall and weighs about 110 pounds. When she was just out of high school, she met and married Reuben Brue.

Reuben wanted to start his own trucking company. He bought a truck and began hauling gravel and sand. To grow their business, yet save money and invest as best they could, they bought another truck, which meant they had to find another driver. Bernice decided she could be that driver.

At the age of 19, this gorgeous, petite lady began driving a gravel truck every day, sometimes six or seven times a week, to grow the trucking company that her husband envisioned. This is a woman who will talk about those days of her marriage and her work with nothing but smiles and gratitude and positive memories. Think that through for a minute. Here's a tiny woman driving a gravel truck on mostly gravel roads to and from gravel pits and sand pits without air-conditioning in sometimes 80, 90, and maybe even 100 degree weather. Her great attitude never wavered.

To this day, even at 87 and walking with a walker, this is a woman who never has a bad word to say. She never has a negative comment. I don't know that she's ever had a bad day, in spite of going through a bankruptcy of the business and in spite of losing her husband to heart failure. She raised four wonderful kids and she is the epitome of a person who finds the best in every day and loves life.

What can we learn from Bernice? We all have had bad days and bad weeks, and we might even have had bad years. But she shows it's possible to love life.

You may be thinking that Bernice is just one of those people who were born happy, and that may be true. Psychologists agree that happiness depends to a great extent on the "happiness set point," a genetically determined feeling of optimism and well being that is "normal" for an individual. However they also acknowledge that nearly as important are the deliberate actions we take toward increasing our happiness level. In 1991, Martin Seligman, Ph.D., often called the "Father of Positive Psychology," said, "Habits of thinking need not be forever. One of the most significant findings in psychology in the last twenty years is that individuals can choose the way they think."

Consider the Attitude Factor

If you are 55 and hate your job, give some thought to what your mood and your attitude are before you conclude that the problem is the boss, the job, or the company.

Tom was very dissatisfied when I met him and he complained about his work incessantly. He always had something negative to say about the people he worked with or about his boss. He would say he wasn't getting paid enough money. I remember one day he complained about the telephone systems not working. "How can anybody work in an environment without a phone?" he railed. That phone outage only lasted three hours. There was always something.

As I worked with Tom, I realized that he really did like the work that he did. The people that he worked with really weren't bad, and his work environment wasn't bad. Tom just had an attitude that everything was negative. If you are familiar with the character Eeyore in *Winnie the Pooh* books, you would see that Tom had Eeyore's "woe is me" attitude.

As I coached Tom, we spent an enormous amount of time working on attitude. I spent the first three or four sessions just listening and taking notes. Letting Tom vent helped some. I wrote down his complaints verbatim. When I felt like I had enough information, I went back to Tom and we started discussing certain specific incidents and situations. We delved into what happened, what made that situation so bad. Was life really so horrible? Was an incident so bad that it was ruining the rest of his day? Did all the complaining mean anything?

Tom eventually came to his own conclusion, over a period of time, that none of those things in and of themselves were all that bad. They were inconveniences, or they were very short-term setbacks. Over a period of time, Tom realized that he was ruminating over little things. He realized the rumination was a bad habit he could change. Thinking about the book *Don't Sweat the Small Stuff*, Tom came to his own conclusion that he was sweating the small stuff.

Recognizing that your negative attitude is making your work life more difficult allows you to consider ways that you can replace your negative thoughts with positive alternatives.

Taking a positive look at the incidents he experiences at work was just one technique that Tom and I employed. Tom also improved his attitude by looking for alternatives to some of the situations that bothered him. When I asked Tom what would be better options for him to pursue, he realized there was no alternate situation that he would like better. Tom wasn't interested in taking a new job or even substantially changing the job he has. By reflecting on the reality of his situation over a period of time, Tom came to his own conclusion that things weren't so bad after all.

We made some significant headway. I can't say that Tom wakes up every day as happy as Bernice and feeling that life is just beautiful, but he decided to keep his position and has stayed with his employer three more years at this point.

Is Your Attitude Based on Unrealistic Expectations?

Sometimes before you can improve your attitude, you have to figure out the basis for it. When I started working with a client named Darryl, it appeared that he was very dissatisfied with his job. He was considering leaving the company. When we looked at his work, it was clear that he was in a job that he had been educated to do. The position was true to the job description he had accepted.

Darryl had been happy to accept the job with a well-respected company. Once on board, Darryl had been assigned to a rather routine project. It was not one of the more prestigious or glamorous projects that he would have preferred. Darryl's project supported the main project.

As he looked at working as part of a team, he granted that some of the projects that are more in the background are vital to making the company successful. When we talked about the lead project and the person who was in the lead role, it quickly became apparent that the person in that role was ten years Darryl's senior with a very different background. He had more experience with much more customer interaction and, quite frankly, was more qualified. Darryl came to the realization that, as much as he wanted that other opportunity, he wasn't qualified to do it—yet.

We set in motion a program including an educational component to prepare him to handle the role he wants. The next time an opportunity comes up, Darryl will be ready. The result is that he not only became qualified to move up, but he also enjoys his current role a lot more. He became happier in his position for two reasons:

- He was preparing to do something that he really wanted to do.

- He was going after a goal as opposed to doing his job on a day-in day-out basis.

There is a lesson to be learned here. You probably will enjoy your career more if you keep reaching for the next opportunity. Realizing that what you are doing now is preparing you for the next goal—the next objective you set for yourself—makes the present more positive.

Darryl exemplified the idea that your attitude is related to your expectations. If you have unrealistic expectations, it's easy to become frustrated.

Our work allowed Darryl to see his expectations in a different way. His attitude was a result of unrealistic expectations. If you hate your job because you are not getting the recognition or opportunities you seek, you need to consider your expectations. You also can take charge of your career by identifying your next career goal and preparing to reach it.

Some have greatness thrust upon them.

William Shakespeare

Unrealistic goals that play havoc with someone's attitude often come not from the employee but from management. It is quite possible to develop a bad attitude or become frustrated because an unrealistic goal has been thrust upon you.

One of my clients, Rita, is dealing with just such a goal. Her manager has set a goal for her to increase her top-line revenue by 60%. Achieving such an increase seems so far away and so unattainable that Rita feels beaten down before she even starts.

Considering the challenge of trying to attain that 60% increase, I advised Rita to set some short-term goals. We developed one or two attainable goals per month. They weren't necessarily easy but they were possible and they gave Rita's team something to "high five" about. We brought in two new salespeople who we knew would be revenue generators. These employees helped the team increase their monthly forecast by 25%.

For Rita to look constantly at that 60% year-end goal became too much. It just didn't work for her. Setting up weekly and monthly attainable goals for Rita and her team gave them something to celebrate as opposed to feeling defeated for the entire year.

The other idea we talked about, and this was very difficult, was just trying to enjoy the trip. It's a little like saying I need to drive from Chicago to Los Angeles. The thought of driving more than 2,000 miles can be overwhelming. But if you pick out a few enjoyable things to do along the way—a nice restaurant, hotel, or interesting site to visit—the trip becomes more attractive. You enjoy the scenery along the way; you look at and enjoy the different atmosphere in Kansas City, Oklahoma, and Arizona.

So while you are working your tail off trying to make your 60% goal, consider having a nice lunch with a client, maybe a golf game on a beautiful day. Enjoying the good that might be found in any day makes that difficult goal less depressing.

While Rita struggled to meet the 60% goal, she had the opportunity to develop a different management style. Rita also found it necessary to delegate responsibilities to people on her team, which allowed them to develop new skills. In this situation, all of a sudden, people grew and surprised her with the abilities that she didn't know they had. Even unrealistic expectations from the top down can have positive results along the way.

The Choice Is Yours

If you think that a negative attitude may be contributing to your frustration with your job, it's time to take action. This is a time when a career or life coach may be a great collaborator to help you find the positivity you need to love your job. It also helps to seek out and spend time with friends and colleagues who also try to take a positive view of business and life.

Chapter 4

Financial Factors

How Much Is Enough?

G reg is only 51 and he is feeling unfulfilled in his work. He is the vice president of wealth management for a large bank in the Chicago area. He's frustrated because he does not feel challenged in his career. He does not feel that he is challenging his current company through his role either.

Working with Greg, we spent a long time talking about where that frustration is coming from, how it feels, and why he feels that way. We struggled to figure out how Greg arrived where he is at this point in his career. All of a sudden it became very obvious; Greg realized that the frustration stemmed from feeling he had been wimpy in his job. He said he needed to get bolder—gutsier.

"I feel like I am working day by day doing everything in 'safe mode.' I am taking the safe way in everything—from an organizational standpoint to the setting of goals and objectives for myself and my team. And I am not going to my boss with a proposal for new ways to do business."

There is a time to play things safe, but the safe way is obviously causing that feeling of frustration. I asked Greg what he would do if the company was Greg, Inc. His ideas poured out like a volcano. He would start by reorganizing his team. He would change work assignments and set new goals and objectives. Even though these changes would probably upset some people and stir up some politics, Greg was convinced the company would run more efficiently and effectively.

Greg went on to say, "I don't necessarily want to deal with those office politics. Reorganization would threaten some peoples' jobs and departmental responsibilities, and it would require other people to do more work than they are currently doing. We're talking about an organization that has some 8,000 people. Besides being risky, it is also an awful lot of work. I have a really good thing going on as things are right now.

"I have a beautiful $1.5 million house up north, I have a gorgeous three bedroom home on a golf course in Arizona, I've got a great country club membership here in Chicago. I drive a Porsche, my kids are going to private school, I've set my two daughters up in business for themselves. I just don't want to screw everything up."

So that is what it came down to. He was frustrated because he was not stretching or challenging himself for fear of losing the financial security that he had in his current role. He would most likely enjoy the challenge of trying to do things differently, but changing the status quo is risky.

Greg is basically bored because he's doing the same thing the same way every day even though he believes there's a better way of doing it. He is being held financial hostage by the things that he owns and the lifestyle he enjoys.

Has Your Big Salary Become a Ball and Chain?

If you are 55 and hate your job, you may identify with Greg's frustration. The solution is to figure out whether you want to do your job the way you're doing it for the next 10 years or whether you want to take some risks. Change almost always brings risk.

You may be able to make changes in your job that will improve the company's efficiency and profitability. But if your plans don't work out, you risk the financial structure that your lifestyle depends on. Worst case scenario: let's say you were fired. How hard would it be to find another job that would offer you the same compensation?

If you are not willing to swallow all your frustration and just keep doing the same job in the same way until that happy day when you can retire, you know you have to do something. You have to make a plan.

In his article, *"Being Held Financial Hostage,"* financial planning expert David L. Blaydes recommends creating a plan for your financial future. Taking a realistic look at where you are financially and where you hope to be at retirement age allows you to see your options for keeping or changing your career.

In the following excerpt from *"Being Held Financial Hostage,"* Blaydes shows how to develop a personal blueprint to help you to throw off financial shackles.

Personal Blueprint

Working with a qualified career coach or a financial life planner to create a personal goals-based financial plan will allow Greg to start living life based on design instead of default. The elements of the Blueprint are:

Values: Certain things are important to you, but are you living those values day in, day out?

Meaningful Purpose: What are you "called" to do that will be remembered long after you're gone?

Compelling Vision: How can you achieve success and significance if you don't know what they look like?

Personal Mission: Once you know where you're trying to go, wouldn't it be easier to get there with a map?

Goals (specific, measurable, achievable, compatible): Wouldn't it be helpful to track your progress along the way?

Once the blueprint is completed or at least started, which can be done by either a coach or a financial advisor who uses such a process as the foundation of their financial planning, you need to find a qualified financial professional to assist you with your planning.

Blaydes' complete article is available in the Appendix. It takes you through the financial planning process. Having a solid financial plan in place can give you the confidence to entertain all the options available to you.

Vince Daniels, vice president of human resources for Rheinhold Foods, says, "Only when you know you can leave is when you can stay in a better way."

How Do You Break Through to Personal Freedom?

If you are in a high-paying position, you may be very reluctant to give up that security and comfort zone. But if you take a look at your lifestyle and see that you are spending every penny you earn on things that are not making you happy, you might want to reconsider your lifestyle.

My client Andrew had been a partner in a company for 25 years. He earned what he called "a heck of a lot of money" and was able to support his family in grand style, but he felt like he was living in the movie *Groundhog Day.* Every day seemed the same as the one before.

Andrew elected to leave that organization, sell his stock, and start a consulting and coaching practice where he could do what he wanted to do. In his new position he felt less pressure and was able to spend more time with his family. A move like Andrew's is not for everybody. It's a bold move with no guarantees. You may not be fed up enough with your job to take the plunge and start a new business. There are also options to stay in your current position and change some opportunities and responsibilities to make life more interesting and rewarding.

Jumping ship and starting a new business was not an option that wealth manager Greg could do easily. As we continued to work together, Greg revealed an additional reason why he held back on proposing new strategies to the CEO. The last three people who filled the role he has now had all been fired.

That record of previous VPs of wealth management added significant risk to the options open to Greg. Pressed for the reason for their firing, Greg explained that his predecessors were all fired because they weren't growing the business.

Taking that record into account, Greg's decision became fairly easy. He could stay in his current safe mode, doing the same things the last three wealth managers did, and risk getting fired. Or, he could initiate change.

This is how Greg saw some possible plans for moving forward:

- I can continue to work in safe mode and be bored for the rest of my career and risk getting fired because I didn't make any changes.

- I can write a strategy and a set of goals and objectives that offer a return on investment with an associated timeline. I can present it to my boss and hope to get it approved. Then my risk is lower because now my boss has bought into it.

- The boss can say "no" to my proposal leaving me to decide whether I'm going to stay here in a job that doesn't require me to challenge or be challenged.

- I may need to move to a different organization.

Greg and I talked about what he might be willing to give up in order to leave his current job. Asked if his family might buy into a simpler lifestyle, he said that he and his wife had a conversation about his being bored at work. He mentioned giving up all the "stuff" that they had. She said to him, "Greg, I don't need any of this. I don't need a country club. I don't need a house in Arizona. I don't need a million and a half dollar house. I just want you to come home in a good mood every day and spend more time with the family and be happier. If you're happier, I'm happier. I don't need all these things."

That reaction confirmed that Greg was the one who was attached to the material things. The trappings of wealth look like success to a lot of people. Knowing he was the one attached to the "stuff" his salary provided, Greg felt comfortable downsizing a little. He also felt more comfortable with risk. He decided to risk shaking things up in his current job by proposing a new strategy and new goals and objectives that offered a return on investment and brought new energy into his career.

Aha Moments, Finding True Wealth

Business owner Jacob was diagnosed with stage iv colon cancer at the age of 45. Not only was he making really good money at that point in his life, but he was making really good money for his own company. When he was diagnosed with colon cancer, he literally couldn't work. He had to close his business. He was told that he had about three months to live.

The upside of this story is that he beat colon cancer and he's been cancer free for five years now. Jacob is also one of the happiest human beings I know. Once he regained his health, he started up his business again and is still working. He doesn't make the amount of money that he made before. He resumed his life with a completely different attitude. He has new priorities about time spent at work, time with family and friends, and the way that he enjoys life.

Jacob's new outlook has him spending less money now on fewer tangible things and more on experiential things. He has decided that for him, anyway, he doesn't need a bigger home, he doesn't need a second home, he doesn't need fancier cars. He wants to spend more time with his wife and kids.

Jacob now enjoys spending time on fairly exotic vacations and doing the activities he loves. In the past, he might have gone skiing once or twice a year for a long weekend. He now can go skiing for a week or 10 days at a time three or four times a year. He has taken up bicycling and he may take a 1,500 mile cross-country trip because he loves riding.

To Jacob every day is a gift. Coming so close to death led him to shift priorities. All of it was due to his health, but it certainly impacted him financially. He just chose to look at it from a different angle. He has revised his attitude about his financial planning as well. He is careful to balance saving for retirement with enjoying some of the things money can buy while he and his family are young and healthy.

Enjoying the Trip

Perhaps you can adjust your goals and objectives—or at least how you pursue them—to enjoy your life more. Maybe you look at smaller wins as opposed to bigger wins. Maybe you don't completely reorganize your department and say you're going to grow it by 40%, but you say you're going to tweak it by a couple of key players and grow it by 20%.

Sometimes a career decision becomes a family decision. If you are making changes to your career plan or financial plan, you may need to tell your kids, "Look, I'm going to leave my current employer so I can do something I would rather be doing. In this situation we can't afford Notre Dame's tuition. I'm sorry, but we need to look at some other options."

Sometimes your impending career decision seems overwhelming because you are so close to the situation. Taking a step back and looking at the big picture along with the family can be a comfort. A smaller house or giving up some toys in exchange for a happier spouse or parent may be seen as an easy tradeoff.

It Might Not Be Easy

It's a beautiful thing if you can get to an "enlightened" frame of mind like cancer survivor Jacob. It's not easy to do and it's not possible for everyone to afford trips and vacations. The reality is that college and retirement are both expensive. You have to take your own circumstances into account. A qualified financial planner can be a great resource when you are making career and financial decisions. In the following excerpt from Blaydes' article, *"Being Held Financial Hostage,"* the author offers guidance on how to choose a financial planner.

How to Select a Financial Planner

Credentials: You want to work with an advisor who has financial planning credentials so that the advice is more likely to be financial planning-based than just sales- and/or commission-based. The more notable credentials are:

- CFP™: Certified Financial Planner
- RFC: Registered Financial Consultant
- AIF: Accredited Investment Fiduciary
- MS: Masters in Financial Planning

History: In addition to credentials, you should also check the disciplinary history of the advisor. This can be accomplished by conducting a "broker check" with Financial Industry Regulatory Authority FINRA, the industry's regulatory agency (www.finra.org).

Area of specialty: Just as you would go to a cardiologist instead of a dermatologist for heart-related issues, you should go to an advisor who specializes in your area of need. An advisor who specializes in working with individuals as they prepare for a job change or retirement is different from one who specializes in working with business owners.

Experience: Just as you would be hesitant to go to a doctor fresh out of med school, a financial advisor with a couple decades of experience is advisable.

> *Personal comfort level:* To keep the doctor theme going, we could call this the financial planner's bedside manner. While it may not feel very-important, you want to work with someone you're comfortable withso that you're more likely to return for annual reviews to keep your financial plan current.

Blaydes' complete article is available in the Appendix.

Disclosure

1. *Opinions voiced in this chapter/Appendix are not intended to provide specific advice and should not be construed as recommendations for any individual. To determine which investments may be appropriate for you, consult with your financial, tax, or legal professional. Please remember that investment decisions should be based on an individual's goals, time horizon, and tolerance for risk. Furthermore, any listing of a vendor or product does not constitute an endorsement or warranty of the vendor or product by the National Planning Corporation (NPC). NPC is not to be held responsible for and may not be held liable for the adequacy of the information available. David Blaydes, Retirement Planners International, Inc. and NPC are separate and unrelated companies.*

2. *Asset allocation strategies are designed in an effort to optimize risk and reward, but cannot guarantee a profit or protect against a loss.*

3. *All examples used are for hypothetical illustration only, not indicative of any particular investment, actual results will vary.*

4. *Security and advisory services offered through National Planning Corporation (NPC), Member FINRA/SIPC, a Registered Investment Adviser. RPI, Inc. and NPC are separate and unrelated companies.*

What About You?

How long has it been since you have done a reality check on your lifestyle? How important is it to you that you maintain your status quo regarding your home(s), cars, vacations, boats and other toys? How important are those things to your family? Could you all be just as happy with fewer things and less pressure?

Chapter 5

Philanthropy and Passion

Put Your Energy Where Your Heart Is

A t the age of 12, my son was diagnosed with Crohn's disease. When your child is sick, you want to do anything you can to make his life better. That's certainly the way I felt. It wasn't practical for me to think I would go back to school and study medicine so I could research Crohn's and colitis, or gastrointestinal diseases. But I wanted to do something, so I went on a charity walk to help create awareness and to raise money for Crohn's research. Shortly after participating in that walk, I became involved in managing the walk.

I was invited to join the board of the Crohn's and Colitis Foundation of America, and eventually I served as the president of the board for three years. I was passionate about supporting education and research efforts of the CCFA. At the same time, I was very philanthropic, supporting that organization with my time and money. I felt good about what I was doing for my son, and I also felt good about what I was doing for me and how I was participating in his healing.

My passion to help that foundation made an impact on my feelings about myself and my feelings about my work and my life purpose.

At that point in my life, I can say that my volunteer work was as important to me as my career. Since then I have learned that volunteer work often has a profound effect on volunteers.

Philip Moeller, one of the authors of *How to Live to 100*, quoted Linda Fried, a professor of public health at Columbia University Medical Center:

"The...thing that is really important to people, particularly as they get older, is that they feel they've made a difference being on the planet," Fried says. "That's a deeply personal sense of meaning, particularly as people take stock of their lives."

If you are 55 and hate your job, you may begin to feel that the only way to improve your life is to quit your job. That might be one way to change your life, but it may not be the best way.

This would be a good time to take a look at how you are using your days. If work is all you do and that is not providing satisfaction, you might consider rearranging your priorities. Before you jump ship and look for a new job, think about what interests, experiences, and causes you are passionate about. I recommend you look for ways outside of work to follow your passion. You may find that those activities will enrich your life and lower your stress and frustration. Just as we encourage children to be "well rounded" during their school years, it's healthy to apply that same wisdom to our own lives.

I think passionate endeavors and philanthropy are critical to our happiness. When you act on your highest intentions, your happiness expands to include your personal life, your work life, your family, and your relationships.

In her book, *The How of Happiness,* Sonja Lyubomirsky, Ph.D., states,

One study followed women with multiple sclerosis (MS) who volunteered as peer supporters to other patients. They received training in compassionate listening techniques and called the patients to talk and listen for 15 minutes at a time. The study followed the volunteers for three years and found that they had increased self-esteem, self-acceptance, satisfaction, self-efficacy, social activity, and feelings of mastery. The positive outcomes for the volunteers were even greater than for the patients they were helping.

I would say the same thing is certainly true for those who reach out outside of their work to do something that they're passionate about, whether it is flying an airplane or volunteering at a food bank. Most people who volunteer or financially support a cause report they feel they receive more than they give. It's hard to quantify the rewards of volunteering. The CEO of a Fortune 100 company may only manage to volunteer two days a year at a food bank at his or her church, but the reward of meeting the other volunteers and the people the food bank serves may fill the executive with the empathy and humility to look at the world a little differently. That might be the beginning of a new leadership style in the CEO's career.

Getting on the Philanthropy Bandwagon at Work

If you are 55 and hate your job, you might look around to see if your company has a presence on the philanthropic landscape that appeals to you. Many companies have a partnership with certain causes or charities in their local community and/or on a global level.

Ellen Costello, former CEO of Harris Bank and head of the U.S. holding company of BMO Harris, said that 950 of the BMO Harris' 1,250 senior management people are involved on boards of directors of philanthropic organizations. She revealed that the company not only supports that involvement, they encourage it. It's not just because BMO Harris wants to be known as a huge philanthropic organization. She believes that the company is equally motivated by the belief that by serving on not-for-profit boards and giving back to the community in meaningful ways, senior managers become better leaders. They become more understanding of people, have more empathy, and develop greater respect and appreciation for what they have both at home and at work.

I admire the insight of CEOs who value their employees' volunteer time and realizes that the company benefits by having employees who are aware and involved in the community.

When Employees Give, Everybody Wins

Some corporations have formal volunteer programs in place that provide opportunities for employees who aren't already committed to a cause. If you are 55 and hate your job, you might find that getting involved in a corporate-sponsored volunteer effort improves your job satisfaction.

If your company doesn't have a formal philanthropy or volunteer program, you might be able to convince management to support your philanthropic ideas. Human Resources and senior management have a strong vested interest in employee engagement, and studies show that employees involved in corporate volunteering are more engaged in their careers.

An Overworked Executive Changes Her Focus

If you decide that pursuing volunteer work outside of your job is the way you would like to refocus your energy, the following example might inspire you.

Jennifer was an executive with a Fortune 500 company who became dissatisfied with her work. Her heavy workload left little time for anything else in her life. She was feeling overextended, overwhelmed, and frustrated. She went to her manager and said, "Look, I'm working 65-75 hours a week and I need to make some changes. I really want to spend more time volunteering at a shelter for battered women."

She had done her homework and figured out what she wanted her workweek to look like. "I would like to work a four-day workweek. Then I could work evenings and some of my weekends in the shelter." Her management responded positively. Not only did they respect her desire to support the shelter, but they wanted to keep her in her professional role in some capacity.

I think companies are more open to proposals like this than you may think. A lot of times people believe that they need to completely exit their company and turn their life upside down to do something different. They may be surprised at their organization's willingness to support their desire to give back. It's a gutsy decision to go to your company and say you don't want to continue the status quo anymore. There is a risk of being told, "Well, if you don't want to do it, we're going to find somebody else who will."

You have to be smart and strategic as you plan how to approach your organization, but I think there are many organizations out there that are willing to cooperate with your philanthropy. As the American workforce ages, companies have come to value the institutional knowledge that is walking out the door with retirees. If a valued employee is dissatisfied, management may be willing to negotiate to keep some of that institutional knowledge on board, even if it is on a part-time basis.

Staying with Your Employer in a Different Capacity

Some 55-year-olds who hate their jobs might find a better fit in the same company by changing their responsibilities. I have a good friend who is an attorney who acted as the managing director in a law firm for years, managing the legal practice of hundreds of lawyers. He felt he had become more of a business person than an attorney for the last ten or more years in his career.

As he began looking back on much of his career and his life, he recalled he had gone to college with the dream of becoming a lawyer. He had known from a very early age that he really wanted to practice law and he missed doing that work.

He decided he would go to the management at his company and say, "I would like to begin the process of transitioning away from the managing partner role of this firm. I would like to go back to being a lawyer."

He stayed in his current organization and now he's practicing law, which is what he really wanted to do from the start. He's having more fun now than he had in the last five or ten years of his career. He doesn't miss the management hassles of running a practice.

An Ohio State Alumnus Downsizes His Life

Sometimes dissatisfied employees do have to leave their current jobs to follow their passion and have to make financial plans in order to make that change. We all have financial obligations and responsibilities that sometimes seem to conspire to keep us where we are. If you want to change gears and follow your passion down a new career path, you need to plan ahead.

Steve, a native of Ohio and a graduate of The Ohio State University, wanted to move back to Columbus, Ohio, and teach at the university. He planned ahead so that he would be able to meet his financial responsibilities on a professor's salary that was considerably lower than the executive salary he earned in business. He didn't mind the reduced income because he was fulfilling a dream of "giving back" by doing something he longed to do—to teach at his alma mater. Making this career change fits Steve's personality and he is glad to do it.

Leaving the Wrong Job to Enjoy the Right Life

Some changes are more drastic than that of an executive becoming a professor, but ultimately you are the only one who can decide what career is really right for you.

Mel is a good friend whose father groomed and mentored him into the family business. Unfortunately his father passed away at an early age. Mel took over the business and ran it. Quite frankly, he just wasn't the right person for that job. He was not his dad. He was not a guy who wanted to run a business, manage people, and work with P & L statements. His role required him to manage inventory, oversee sales, and entertain clients, none of which came naturally to him. Because his father "left him the business," his sense of responsibility and a certain amount of guilt kept him in that leadership role.

On top of that, Mel lived in the Midwest and he really didn't like the cold winters. Once his children graduated from high school, he sold everything. I mean everything—his house and his business. He packed up and moved to Florida. He sells real estate part-time and spends his free time fishing and boating. He changed his entire life.

Mel also made the decision that life isn't about being rich. He down-sized extensively. While running the family business, he had two big houses, brand new cars, and all the trappings of success. Many would say he was "living the dream." Now he lives much more simply in a very small condo. He is not driving new cars and not living the lifestyle he had before. However, he is living where he wants to be and doing what he wants to do because he made the decision to change his life.

Creating a New Career

As you have seen, sometimes following a passion does lead to a new job. The following example describes another business owner who followed his dream into a different lifestyle.

My friend Eric started a company right after he graduated from college. He had a couple of partners; they started small but grew the business into a very large company. After a while, Eric found that, rather than managing the business, the business was almost managing him. The responsibilities and needs of the business dictated how he was living his life.

It didn't take too long for Eric to realize he wasn't having fun anymore. He had had the most fun as a young entrepreneur, starting a small business, growing it, and mentoring younger people in the organization. Eric decided to sell his interest in the business to his partners.

Now he works in an "incubator group" where entrepreneurs learn how to put their ideas to work starting their own businesses. He is a mentor to new entrepreneurs, grooming them and helping them grow their businesses. In some cases, he invests in their businesses and serves on their boards of directors. He loves advising and coaching young entrepreneurs.

Eric's role in the incubator group enhances his family life as well. Because of the demands of his first company, he and his wife had waited to start a family until they were a little older. His children are now in high school. He has time to coach both of his kids' soccer teams and baseball teams and goes to all their track meets. He's living the life that he wants to live.

Are you living the life you want to live? Does your work align with your passion? If not, can you follow your passion outside of work? Where does your philanthropy fit into your life?

Chapter 6

Flexibility

Stretching Makes You Stronger

The key to sustained happiness, health, and longevity is flexibility.

Ev Durán

If you are 55 and you hate your job, consider whether you have become set in your ways or whether your job has become automatic for you. Complacency and boredom could be at the root of your dissatisfaction with your job. Increasing your flexibility can empower you to bring vitality back to your career. In order to become fit and motivated both physically and mentally, you need flexibility. As I have reached that magic number of 55, I have noticed that I am not as physically flexible as I was 10 or 15 years ago. Even though I have always been active and somewhat athletic, I find that I have to work harder to make sure I don't stiffen up in order to perform athletic functions without hurting myself.

If you think of your athleticism as an analogy for your career, remind yourself that you need to work hard to remain flexible professionally as well as physically. Being open to new ideas in your industry and in your way of doing business is as important now as ever before— maybe more important.

At this point in your career, you probably have moved up in your organization and developed a lot of habits and management techniques that have served you well. Moving into leadership roles requires you to be more flexible all the time to accommodate the kinds of work you do and changes in your peer group as people get promoted, move on to new jobs, or are brought in from outside the company.

Flexible Management Style

There are at least three generations represented in the workplace right now. There are Baby Boomers, Gen Xers, and Millennials. This situation requires us to be creative in our management styles. The Boomers had one particular way of being managed, working, and being at their best, the Gen X group has another, and Millennials have a third way.

The youngest workers in the workplace grew up with the Internet. They take social media for granted and have always communicated through social networking and speaking electronically more often than face to face. No one has written a memo in years. These types of changes have required us to be flexible and there is no stopping now.

Flexibility enables you to enjoy what you are doing and not get too wrapped up in how you are doing things. Change is always a bit uncomfortable at first, but eventually, new methods and tools become familiar. It may fall to you to lead the way for others in your organization to continue to be flexible.

Flexibility is a requirement for survival.

Roger Von Oech,
A Whack on the Side of the Head: How You Can Be More Creative

Both physical and mental flexibility requires us to exercise. John Wooden, the famous UCLA basketball coach, said, "It is what you learn after you know it all that counts." It is important to remember as we get older and think that we know everything about our job, that we can still learn new things and add new management and communication techniques. When you learn new skills, you add value not only to yourself and to your personal creativity, but also to your role in the company and to your team.

In your early career, you were most likely guided and told what to do. First jobs are often repetitive with roles that require little flexibility. With higher-level jobs you may be called upon to be flexible—to think outside the box to solve problems. Increased responsibilities and more creative business ideas keep you energized and not complacent. Albert Einstein said, "Intellectual growth should commence at birth and cease only at death."

As human beings, we should be learning all the time. If you have mastered your job and started working in an automatic pilot mode, that could be the source of your dissatisfaction with your job. I worked with a client named Henry who wanted to spend the last five to eight years of his career in automatic pilot mode. He felt as though he "deserved" that. He had worked hard and wanted to coast. He was the CEO of the company; he owned the majority of the company's stock and wanted to cruise the last few years to retirement. His exit strategy was to sell the company and retire. However, drastic changes in manufacturing forced Henry to rethink his plan. There would be no coasting in the next few years.

Henry had to decide whether he wanted to sell early at a lower price or to stay with the company. If he stayed, he would have to completely change, not only what he was doing, but also the product mix and the manufacturing process. Staying with the company was going to require an immense amount of energy, thinking in new ways, and bringing in new people. He would have to do things significantly differently than he had done for the last 35 years.

Henry decided to stay with his company, make changes, and add new people. He is still moving the company through continuous change, still bringing on new people. Now he is growing his business and, at the same time, adding to its portfolio value. He is into his fifth year of company growth and will not be retiring for a while yet. He is still having fun and he is still taking his company where he wants it to be.

He found through this change process that he got completely re-energized and re-focused. He enjoyed his work again. Rather than coasting, Henry was exercising his brain and learning a new management style. He was working harder than he had in the previous 15 years, and he was enjoying it more than he had probably enjoyed it in that period.

A guarantee in this life: Change!
Flexibility is better than predictability!

Evinda Lepins

I think he feels much younger and much more energized. He also has a much younger team, which was probably a bit of a surprise to him. He realized that the vast majority of his team were either getting ready to retire or could not keep up with new technology and the new way of thinking that's required to keep going. I think that's also keeping him energized and young.

Henry's company is worth much more today than if he had not changed anything. When prospective buyers see a vibrant young workforce with energy and enthusiasm, they will see the company as a great investment opportunity. What had been an old-line manufacturing business is more salable now than it would have been if Henry had been coasting.

The measure of intelligence is the ability to change.

Albert Einstein

Another client, Chelsea, was in her late 40s but was already tired of her role. Since money was not an issue, she planned on simply taking an early retirement, with no idea what she was going to do after that. She was almost 50 and hated her job.

When Chelsea started talking to the CEO about wanting to take early retirement, he told her he had been planning to ask her to take the lead on a project that was very critical to the ongoing business operation. Even though Chelsea was not a technology person, he asked her to take leadership of a very important, highly technical systems project.

The CEO was convinced that, even with little technical knowledge, Chelsea's excellent project management skills would enable her to make the project a success. Those project management skills were key to this project. The team included outside consultants and internal technology people who would select and implement new technology systems over a six-month period.

Chelsea's project management enabled her to:

- Keep people on track

- Keep the project on schedule

- Keep the project on budget

- Make sure nothing fell between the cracks

- Facilitate internal and external communication with:

- Management

- Customer base

- Outside vendors

- Inside employees

- Outside consultants

Because of her skills, Chelsea was able to complete the project successfully ahead of schedule and under budget.

She had forgotten how good she was at project management, implementation, and leadership. This project made her realize that it wasn't working she disliked, but her specific work. Her previous role had become so mundane because she had developed the processes, procedures, and the group that reported to her to the point where her job was getting quite boring. She had developed her area through succession planning and had made her old job obsolete.

Chelsea's new position gave her new life in her career. Her success on this six-month project led her on a new path as the company's designated go-to person nationally, as well as globally, for projects of all kinds. Her responsibilities included new product development, marketing projects, operations implementation, and even high-level sales strategic growth.

Chelsea, now age 52, is doing project management internally on a consulting basis with her company but also externally on her own. In a few years, she will probably transition out of the company to do her own consulting assignments with her company as well as other companies. She has completely re-energized her work style through her flexibility and openness to doing something different. Now she is taking on new assignments and opening up her thinking about how she will proceed in her career.

The new systems assignment gave Chelsea an awareness of her true skills, which are project management and leadership. She had been in Human Resources and felt that her HR skills were getting stale. The entire area of HR was no longer energizing to her and she had automated a lot of the work in her department.

Most of the groundwork for her to change roles had been done, and Chelsea became open and flexible to take on a project management job in an area in which she had no training. Her flexibility allowed her to contribute to the organization beyond her old role and to re-energize and reinvigorate her career.

Not everyone is fortunate enough to have a CEO give them a new assignment that opens their eyes the way Chelsea's did. But rather than wait for such an opportunity to present itself, you can be proactive by using the "Awareness" skill you will learn in Chapter 7. If you hate your current job, pay attention to the skills you used in past jobs or training, and your skills that you have not yet used. Also, make yourself aware of any opportunities to use different skills, work with different people, or learn new skills within your current company.

Another client, Larry, attended a meeting where a speaker with a healthcare background explained how he was forced to think of creative ways to cut his internal costs. He needed nurses to fill call center positions for his company. He was able to outsource those positions to registered nurses in the Philippines who are willing to work for 20% of the rates of U.S. nurses.

Hearing the speaker, Larry realized he might use labor in other countries in a similar way. In an old, stodgy business where things had not changed in the last 30 to 40 years, Larry looked into outsourcing for his own service business. He spent a week in the Philippines hiring and training people to be outside consultants. His consultants in the Philippines agreed to salaries of $20 per hour; they were very professional and good at what they did. They replaced nine people in the U.S. that he was paying $120 per hour, and Larry was able to pass that savings on to his clients. That made him the low-cost provider in his industry, gave him a leg up on his competition, and created a margin that allowed him to add money to his own bottom line. He created a cost savings for his customers and profit for himself. Within a one-week period, Larry's willingness to be open not only created a five-fold savings for his customers but also improved the profitability of his business.

I think that a motivated "old dog" can learn new tricks. It just takes the flexibility to be open-minded and practice positivity and persistence. You can reinvigorate yourself. You can create ways to like what you do so that you don't wind up being 55 and hating your job.

The key word here is "positivity." In my coaching practice I see that having a positive attitude and upbeat style is an important characteristic of leadership. It is very rare that a person with a negative attitude becomes a leader in any organization. Show me a positive person with average intelligence and average skills, and show me a negative person with highly developed intelligence and skills, and I will bet that the positive person will ultimately be the leader.

Physical Fitness Can Jump-start a Stalled Career

Research shows that a physical workout releases endorphins, the feel-good hormone, which, in turn, increases energy and creativity. So exercise not only enhances your mental and physical health, but in the process, creates a higher level of confidence. When you have a high level of confidence, you're more willing to take risks. When you are more willing to take risks, you create more adrenaline and more excitement and more fun and have the ability to think outside the box. All of that is backed up by research. The creation of endorphins causes not only physical change, it also generates mood-altering mindsets. This sets off a whole chain of events that result in the benefits we have been talking about.

Kim Ravida is a business coach who also has a background in health and fitness. She often sees her clients improve their fitness and career situations in tandem. She tells the success story of her client Bruce. Bruce was in his 50s when he came to her saying he just wasn't happy. He had been in his engineering job with a large corporation for many years and had a side business reviewing drawings by other engineers.

Bruce's doctor had just told him he needed to start taking medications for high blood pressure, diabetes, and high cholesterol. Bruce asked for time to see if he could improve his health on his own before trying the prescriptions.

Working with Kim, the first thing Bruce did was to become aware that he had too much sugar in his diet. As with many people with a high carb diet, he usually had an afternoon slump at work. Bruce began taking a walk around the office and substituting a glass of water in the afternoon for his customary coffee and cookie. He noticed a definite improvement in his energy and mood with that change. He also had a chance to talk informally with colleagues as he walked around and they were able to discuss and resolve a lot of questions in person rather than through email and phone calls.

After a few weeks, Bruce started adding a walk outside to his routine after lunch. Two colleagues joined him in these walks.

When Bruce returned to his doctor, he found that his weight, blood pressure, cholesterol, and blood sugars were in a healthy range so that he was able to avoid starting medicines for those issues. What's more, Bruce felt more energized and motivated to market his own business and create a plan to transition from his corporate job to becoming a full-time entrepreneur.

What's your next move? Do you need more flexibility in how you do your current job? Do you need to be more open to different possible assignments in your company? Would making some new health choices re-energize you at work and in your life?

Chapter **7**

Awareness,
Acknowledgement, &
Appreciation

Creating an A Team

Travel with Someone You Trust!

Since I have always been a car guy, I became aware of AAA (American Automobile Association) when I was growing up in the small town of Ottawa, Illinois. I knew that members of AAA could count on help anytime they had a problem with their car or travel plans.

The idea of AAA being a source for information and support stuck with me and led me to think of AAA as a formula for behavior change. For me, AAA stands for Awareness, Acknowledgement, and Appreciation.

> *What is necessary to change a person
> is to change his awareness of himself.*

Abraham Maslow, psychologist

Awareness, acknowledgement, and appreciation come into play in your career in two ways. The first is in relation to your own current situation. The second is how awareness, acknowledgement, and appreciation affect your relationships with others in your company.

AAA in Your Own Career

If you are 55 and you hate your job, awareness is the first step to making a positive change in your life. Becoming aware means you have to figure out whether:

- You really do hate your job

- There is something going on within the company that makes you think you hate your job

- There is something going on in your life that makes you think you hate your job

Until you become aware of the root problem, it's really hard to solve it. Once you become aware of why or what is causing you to feel the way you do, then you can work on a solution. You have to thoroughly acknowledge and come to grips with the problem in order to figure out how to deal with the reality. Finally, you must appreciate the fact that you have to choose either to do something about it, or not. Your appreciation comes through maintaining a positive attitude and applying it to the process of change.

> *Always leave your campsite better than you found it.*

Old Camping Adage

As a member of the Boy Scouts when I was a kid, I learned the old camping adage: "Always leave the campsite better than you found it." To do that, you have to be aware of what that campsite looked like when you showed up. You need to make a conscious decision to pay attention. Then you have to make it better when you leave. If there was trash in the fire pit, or the ground wasn't raked out properly, or people didn't take care of the campsite, it's your job to make it better before you leave.

Considering jobs and careers, if you view your job as your campsite, you might better appreciate what it takes to leave that job or that company better than it was when you first got there. It's not just about going to work every day from eight to five and doing your job. It's not just about getting something done to add value, or profitability, to the company. It really can go much deeper than that. I think you get a higher level of personal satisfaction if you look at the entire job as you look at the campsite. If you become deeply aware of how it was when you got there, you become aware of what you can do to:

- Leave it in a better situation than when you got there
- Prepare somebody to take over for you when you leave

This practice alone could make you feel a lot better about your job because you now have a new motivation. The light at the end of the tunnel is preparing you either to move on within the company or to move to another opportunity knowing that you left your campsite better than you found it.

I worked with Bob, a vice president of operations for a large manufacturing company. It was a multi-billion-dollar manufacturing company, and Bob just wasn't happy. He didn't seem completely depressed, but he was not a happy guy. He had been VP of operations for nine years, he thought he was getting stale, and he wasn't challenged.

He believed that the president, the CEO of the company, and some members of the board of directors were holding him back. He felt the company was not only holding back his growth but also their own growth. At first Bob wasn't aware that he was just waiting for the president and CEO or the board to come up with big ideas, solutions to big problems, and great new marketing plans. He wanted somebody to come up with a way to make his job more interesting.

Bob and I had some challenging discussions. He came up with hurdle after hurdle that made it impossible for him to change. I kept knocking down the hurdles. He kept coming up with reasons why he was feeling the way he did. There were changes he could have made; he just didn't make them.

The president, the CEO, and the board were not saying no to anything he wanted to do. They weren't disapproving of any plans or formal ideas; he just assumed that they didn't want to make changes because they weren't coming up with ideas. He wasn't aware that his boredom and lack of challenges were within his control.

When we finally got to the cause of his discontent, Bob became aware that he was experiencing a loss of energy and enthusiasm. At the same time, he was really afraid of breaking the mold that he had put together for his role years ago. He had the notion that the company was just clicking along on its own and he hesitated to make waves.

He had done a great job of getting people in place and getting procedures in place to make operations run smoothly. The problem was that he had made his job so automated and efficient that it became mundane and almost unnecessary. In the process of becoming aware of his circumstances, Bob realized that he had a choice to make.

He could:

* Shake up his current job with bigger plans and bigger ideas

* Move on to another job, possibly another company

With greater awareness, Bob came to realize that he liked the company. He came to realize that it wasn't the president or the board who were holding him back. Bob was holding Bob back. Once he became aware of that, he acknowledged that the fun part of his job was when he was new, when he came in with his own new ideas, brought in new people, and implemented policies and procedures. That was when he was in his element. Only after everything became automated did Bob become disillusioned with his job.

Bob acknowledged that he needed to change his behavior, re-engage the old Bob, and come up with new ideas. Or he needed to go to a larger company or a broken company where he could do what he did best. Ultimately, Bob decided to develop a plan for his current company, working with his marketing peer, his sales peer, and the rest of his peer group. When he presented it to the president, the president brought him in with his team of peers to present it to the board of directors. Everybody bought into it.

He is now in the process of making the company a larger, more competitive organization. It looks like he will probably spin off a chunk of this business to create a new subsidiary within the company. This transformation completely re-energized Bob. Through awareness, acknowledgement, and the appreciation of how his own behavior dictated his job satisfaction, Bob was able to re-engage in his job and truly enjoy it again.

Maybe It's Not the Job

Another client, Lori, was a CFO at a large service company. Unfortunately, Lori had gained about 60 pounds over the course of two years. Her health and her energy level were rapidly deteriorating. She was in her early 50s and she was very unhappy at her job and in her personal life as well.

The employees on her team seemed to become less motivated, the organization seemed flat. She noticed people in her organization were coming in later and leaving earlier; projects were getting behind schedule. She felt as though she was working harder (even though she wasn't). The problem was that everything became a huge drain on her energy. Lori was really down and struggling in all areas of her life.

As we worked through what was going on, Lori became aware that she was clinically depressed. She wasn't sleeping at night, she found herself overeating and becoming withdrawn. She reverted to some behaviors from her childhood when she was overweight and was bullied at school. Lori found herself feeling about her company and her employees the same way she had felt about a lot of the kids in school. She had developed a bad attitude. The key to understanding what was going on came when Lori commented that she hadn't felt this way since she was a little girl in grade school and high school.

We started talking about Lori's childhood experiences. That's when she became aware, not only of her depression, but also of her feelings about her company and her feelings about her job. She acknowledged that the time she was happiest in her life was right after college. At that time she was involved in an exercise program and lost a lot of weight. She got married and was very active, even running marathons. Life was good and she was enthusiastic. She grew very quickly in her career.

It became apparent that Lori's good health practices formed the foundation of her success and happiness. When she started to let go of those behaviors, she began to spend more time at work and her life got out of balance.

She recognized that she had reverted to her old unhealthy behavior. The more she ate, the more withdrawn she became, and that became a vicious cycle. Through the awareness and the acknowledgement of her past and current behaviors, she realized that she needed to make changes. She didn't blame the company or her boss for her unhappiness. She began to get her life under control. She started her exercise program again; she lost weight and started feeling good about herself again.

Lori sought treatment from a psychiatrist and received a prescription to help with her clinical depression. She also hired a fitness trainer to keep her exercise program on schedule. She wouldn't miss a workout because she was paying this trainer quite a bit of money. She sought the advice of a dietician and continued to get her life back on track.

Since she became healthier, Lori's life has been on an upswing. She is with the same company and her team members are all pulling together. She is enjoying her job and her coworkers again.

Applying AAA to Others at Work

Appreciation is a wonderful thing. It makes what is excellent in others belong to us as well.

Voltaire

Tim Covey, who mentored me early in my career, was CEO of a manufacturing company and an outstanding manager in a manufacturing environment. He had a great tool that put awareness, acknowledgement, and appreciation to work in his company. He called it his MBWA. He already had an MBA. Then he set about employing MBWA, Management by Walking Around.

The company had an executive dining room, but Tim never ate there. He ate in the cafeteria with the hourly employees, the exempt and non-exempt employees, and salaried employees. He talked to the people around him.

After lunch Tim would walk through the manufacturing plant. Every single day that he was in the office, he ate in the cafeteria and walked around the plant to talk to people.

Tim had a strong awareness of the culture that he had built in the company. He always knew what issues faced the employees in the operations and the manufacturing plant. When he walked around, he would be fully present within the moment and listen.

Tim scheduled walking around time with the same attention he would give to an executive meeting. This was not something he did just once in a while; he spent at least 30 to 45 minutes every day doing MBWA. This practice not only kept his awareness level very high, it also allowed him to acknowledge both the good and bad things the employees faced in their lives. It also allowed him to acknowledge the people who were there and what was going on in their lives, both the good and the bad.

He was on a first-name basis with most of the employees. That allowed him to appreciate the ups and the downs, the highs and the lows of everyone in the organization. He didn't hear only from the senior executives for whom a bad day meant the sprinkler system for their lawn wasn't working right.

MBWA kept him aware of the fact that there were people making hourly wages who were having trouble paying their auto insurance, or sending their kids to college, or paying a medical bill that the insurance didn't cover. That gave him a solid awareness and balanced insight, not only from a corporate perspective as a CEO, but also from a personal perspective as a human being.

He was very philanthropic, giving and empathetic. He was a strong manager and leader. He knew he had to satisfy a board of directors and a senior team. He had to be mindful of profit and loss. His management style didn't make him any less of a negotiator during union contract negotiations. But, it did make him aware of the people who worked in the organization, and it made them aware of him and his challenges.

The best and safest thing is to keep a balance in your life, acknowledge the great powers around us and in us. If you can do that, and live that way, you are really a wise man.

Euripides

I remember an incident that shows the reciprocal awareness, appreciation, and acknowledgement between Tim and the operations employees. Tim was an engineer by education, so he was mechanically inclined. A fellow named Dale was having trouble with a metal stamping machine and no one could fix it. The service technicians said they were going to have maintenance shut it down so they could retool it. The line in the plant that depended on this machine would be down for an extended period of time.

Tim and Dale talked about what was going on. I remember Tim was wearing a white shirt. He took his tie off and started crawling around on the floor. Between Tim and Dale, they were able to get the machine back up and running. The floor around a metal stamping machine is not the cleanest area in the world, and I remember his shirt being covered with oil, grease, and dirt. It had to have been ruined.

This incident made the employees aware of Tim's willingness to get his hands dirty to keep the place up and running. It was evident that Tim appreciated the employeess' frustration with the machine not working. I'm sure the employees who saw this had to be impressed, not only with Tim's ability to get the machine fixed, but also with his willingness to do it. This is just one example of how well Tim related to blue-collar as well as to white-collar employees in the company.

Appreciating Others

If you are 55 and hate your job, sometimes it's hard to remain aware of the other people around you and the effort they are putting into their jobs.

If it's your job to keep others motivated about what they are doing, any improvement you bring to your position by using the three As will help lift up your team, too. "Improving your campsite" will benefit your team and the whole company.

Your improved leadership within the organization will help keep your group motivated and positive so they are coming in on time and not leaving early, and they are excited about what they're doing. That gets back to keeping a total awareness of what is going on and how your group is feeling. As you are acknowledging what they're doing and showing appreciation to them, even though you may not be at 100%, you are making sure they're at 100%.

Do you remember Len the sales manager from Chapter 1? He was clearly a manager who needed to become aware of others on a personal level, appreciate their individual needs and struggles, and acknowledge those needs in the way he led.

Where can you employ awareness, acknowledgment and appreciation to improve your career and relationships with your colleagues?

Chapter **8**

Networking

With Help from Your Friends

I recently heard a speaker talking about the importance of networking and keeping your social and professional network alive. The comment that stuck out for me was, "If you're not networking, you're not working." He meant it ironically, implying that if you do not network, you will ultimately be out of work. He was referring to politics at the office and the need to be networked positively in your job.

I like to think of it a bit differently in that if you are networking and you happen to lose your job, your chances of getting another job will increase and your effort will decrease. You see, over 90% of all jobs secured in the market today are attained through networking. It can be directly through your social network of neighbors, friends, and acquaintances, or it can be indirectly through the use of LinkedIn, organizations to which you belong, professional networks, alumni associations, and the like.

I can offer multiple examples of networking and its importance. However, we already know this. The problem is that it takes time and is not always the most fun thing to do. It can ride low on your priority list and simply get skipped in favor of everything else that is important in your life. I suggest you rethink your priorities and place this simple tool very high on your list.

Let me give you a few examples of this process. I start with a quote from Einstein. When asked what he believed the greatest invention to be, he said, "compound interest." Making money on top of money without having to do much of anything was, in his mind, the greatest invention ever conceived. This is the same guy who figured out $e=mc^2$.

In my mind, networking is another form of compound interest. You meet one person, who introduces you to another, who introduces you to two others, and so on. If you choose to network effectively and then add technology to this equation, with very little effort you can soon have a network of hundreds if not thousands of people. I know of a recruiter who has well over 800,000 contacts on LinkedIn and uses them every day along with her Facebook friends, associates, and other networks to fill searches. Through this continuing process, she gains new contacts, new friends, and new referrals every single day.

I am not suggesting that you do as she does. This is her livelihood and she has taken this to an advanced level. However, we can all learn from her experience. Let me offer up a few examples.

Jack is a gentleman I worked with a few years ago. Jack is extremely bright, almost over-educated, coupled with a less than robust social and emotional intelligence. He is a scientist who loves research and solving statistical problems. Because of his success as an individual contributor at work, he was offered the responsibility of management. Swayed by the money being offered, Jack accepted and quickly failed as a leader and a department head. Jack had very few friends, very few contacts, and had done virtually no networking of any kind.

Jack went to work, went home, and stayed to himself. We first met when he became unemployed. We talked about his career, his next steps, his goals and desires, his passions, and his financial future. Jack was married and had three children at home. His children were rapidly approaching their college years with associated expenses.

I asked Jack to assemble a list of all of his contacts so that we could begin to use the plans we had talked about. Jack came back to my office a few days later with a list of seven people. Four of them were old college professors. Together we decided that in addition to getting him ready to research potential opportunities and interview, we also needed to generate a much broader and deeper list of contacts with whom he could build a network. We also decided that we needed to take some additional time to make these networks meaningful and lasting.

Volunteering, coaching, church, and professional organizations within his expertise were going to be our target. Jack had been a swimmer in college (in the top 20 nationally). He enjoyed his children and working with other children; he had simply never taken time to do this due to his career priorities. Jack was a spiritual guy who left his church years ago for his own reasons. Even though an expert in his field, he never thought it was important to join the associations and organizations that revolved around his expertise and his science.

Fast forward seven months. Jack began to volunteer in a science lab at a local university, working with students and professors, adding tremendous work experience to an otherwise scientific approach to the field. Jack assisted his daughters' swim team and also began his new workout regimen filled with daily swimming. He attended a church in his neighborhood, joined their "Jobs Program" for out-of-work parishioners, and joined two organizations specifically related to his discipline and industry.

What Jack learned was that he actually had a reputation in his field due to products and additives he had developed that were used in other companies and industries. He was quickly becoming a well-known commodity and was sought out for, not only his expertise within his own science, but for his ideas and his creativity in other areas unrelated to his expertise. Jack was becoming a rock star. And... he liked it.

Jack ultimately wound up accepting a position in the research and development department of a very large food company. He continued to teach part-time at his local university and stayed on as an assistant swim coach with the high school even though his youngest child chose not to swim on the team. Jack is a networking phenom. Even though his social skills were not strong, he targeted areas of importance to him, got involved, stepped out of his comfort zone and established a formidable network of friends and professionals.

Another client, Dan, was the CFO of a medium-sized manufacturing company. Dan was an excellent CFO, with good vision and great financial skills. He was a competent manager of his people. His peers liked him and he had 21 years with the same company. In 2012, Dan spent almost an entire year assisting the owner of his company in getting it ready to sell, doing a road show, working with a marketing and advertising firm, and ultimately selling the company. The company was purchased by a large corporation that rolled the business under its existing structure, leaving the finance department along with many others unemployed. Dan was 56 and unemployed.

Dan left with a little money from the owner for his loyalty and his work, but he was not wealthy enough to retire nor did he want to stop working. Dan's spouse was a professional woman who traveled a great deal, his children were almost grown, and they lived on a fairly large piece of property in the country with no neighbors to speak of.

On March 31, Dan found himself sitting at home, unemployed, by himself, with no real hobbies, no outside interests, and no network. In the process of working with Dan, we realized that he would have to develop a resumé, practice his interviewing skills, and get himself ready for a new position with a new company. He also needed to "get a life" and build a network. Dan didn't golf, he didn't fish, he hadn't played sports early on in his life. Other than his family, who were independent, and his work, Dan's only personal interest was playing a guitar given to him by his mother when he was 13. While struggling through his emotional needs, his practical work of finding a job, and his feeling less than useful or appreciated, Dan developed a new love for playing his guitar and music. In the process, Dan realized that he could not only play music but that he could write music and sing (which he had never done in his life).

Dan began to write songs and play them in his basement in a small studio that he built to pass some time when he wasn't interviewing, learning to find a position, or networking. One afternoon, Dan's oldest son, Jacob, heard someone singing and playing "a very cool song." Jacob went downstairs and was shocked to see his father playing and singing like a professional. Jacob and the rest of his family convinced Dan to play at their church and to write a few more songs. The congregation loved Dan's music and he became an almost overnight sensation in a very large church with numerous professional members. Within a matter of weeks, Dan was offered a position as the CFO of a multi-million-dollar manufacturing company, and within two years, he became the COO in line to be the CEO under the succession plan. Dan's newfound musical skills had drawn the attention of the business owner, and his new networking skills allowed him to win that excellent new job.

"If you're not networking, you're not working." Neither Jack nor Dan had any professional network to begin with and they had let their personal networks dry up due to work or family priorities, or simply because they deemed networking unimportant to their careers or lives.

Both of these gentlemen would be quick to tell you that you need a network and if you don't have a network, build one. Once you have your network, keep it very active, spend time on it, and nurture it as a valuable resource for your career and personal life. You will find your network will enhance your personal brand, your discipline, and your outside activities. It can also keep you abreast of changes in your industry. And, if you find yourself in a job search, your network can be a career saver. The thing to remember is that it can dry up quickly, change rapidly, and become old fast. Well-planned physical exercise does nothing if you don't put it into practice. Networking is an exercise that requires discipline, time, and energy in order to keep you at the top of your game. Work it.

Chapter 9

Coaching

It Takes a Coach to Make a Champion

I hope by now the benefits of coaching to an executive's life and business are evident. However, for some of you that require facts and statistics as well as testimonials and articles with third party appraisals, here are some things to consider.

The Financial Times: "Coaching has undergone a U-turn. Gone are the times when sessions with an executive coach were left out of senior diaries. Today's trend is for high-potential employees to be coached or mentored, rather than just those deemed to be underperforming and in need of help—and despite the economic times it is on the rise."

Why is it on the rise? I believe that coaching has finally received the PR and brand that it should have, recognizing its contribution to rising profits, enhanced leadership capabilities, and personal performance. Brad Smart, author of *Top Grading*, should be given credit for proving that hiring and developing "A" players can and does impact stock-holder value, profits, and bottom-line results.

The Chartered Institute of Personnel Development surveyed more than 1,000 people, and they confirmed that, "Coaching and in-house development remain the most effective talent management activities."

Some believe that the change in attitude and the rise in the use of coaching are partly a result of pressures facing business leaders during economic uncertainty. Opportunities to reflect on their performance with a trusted outsider have become a "must." According to a senior HR leader with whom I worked, "When executives are promoted into the most senior leadership positions, they find it more and more difficult to find opportunities to reflect on their leadership and sources of honest feedback become fewer and fewer."

Petra Wilson, director of strategy and external affairs at Chartered Management Institute, says, "Research shows managers rate coaching as one of the top five most effective means of developing management skills. Coaching by external professionals is also well suited to helping senior managers think about the complex challenges they face by providing a new perspective. Many chief executives and senior managers wish they had had coaching earlier in their careers."

A study done by the Boston Consulting Group in July, 2012, made the following conclusion: companies that are serious about their leadership experienced 2.1 times the revenue growth and 1.8 times the profit margin relative to their competitors. Integral Development, based in Perth, Washington, found that, while it is almost impossible to determine an exact Return on Investment (ROI) on executive coaching due to some of the subjective elements associated with it, most studies, no matter what criteria and metrics are employed, arrive at the same conclusion: executive coaching produces an ROI between 500% and 600%. Many different studies have been conducted since 1999, from sources such as *Fortune, Chemistry Business Magazine,* the International Coach Federation, and Linkage, Inc. They all reported an average ROI between five and seven times the amount of the initial investment.

Dr. Ron Cacioppe, Ph.D., managing director at Integral Development, offers his own unique perspective: "Every study that has been conducted in an attempt to determine the ROI of executive coaching has been criticized because many see them as an attempt to compile objective data through subjective means. While the critics have a good point, it certainly doesn't invalidate the data that has been collected since 1999. While there is no methodology in place to assemble irrefutable data, the similarities between results of every divergent methodology used in studies trying to determine a definitive ROI for executive coaching cannot be trivialized. On the surface, the data may appear anecdotal, but every path leads to the same conclusion: an ROI of five to seven times the original investment."

In addition to pure development, coaching can have a tremendously positive impact on an organization's retention. It is a commonly known fact that employees who believe in their organization and its products or services are more productive and loyal. It is also known that employees who believe that their company believes in them are more loyal and, therefore, more apt to stay with the organization. Coaching gives an employee the belief and the confidence that their organization is investing in their future and believes in them as future or existing leaders.

A *Los Angeles Times* article by Richard Lopez reported a Gallup Poll showed that 70% of workers have "checked out" or have become "disengaged." Another study by Development Dimensions International polled more than 1,000 executives and asked if they were actively searching for new employment. The results should be of notice to corporate America. Sixty percent said "yes," 21% said "maybe," 13% said "no," and only 6% said "not likely," but they do have an up-to-date resumé.

I believe that executive coaching has significant positive impacts on both the executives and the organizations who employ them. When I coach an executive client I concentrate on three of the most important principles of a leader: *presence* (being fully engaged), *psychology* (are they living the truth of the organization), *physiology* (caring for themselves physically and emotionally as well as at home).

Just as top athletes rely on the best coaches to push their performance to new heights, CEOs may want to consider executive coaches as vital to "performance enhancement." Heinz CEO Bill Johnson, the son of a former NFL coach of the Cincinnati Bengals, employs one for himself. "Why not?" says Johnson. "Tiger Woods has a coach."

When boards and other stakeholders recognize the value of executive coaching for their C-suite executives, the result can be the difference between having a good organization with good people and having a great organization, with people who come together every day to create real, sustained value.

What kind of coaching would you seek if you were given the opportunity? You don't have to wait for your company to hire a coach for you. You can take charge of your own career and hire a coach to help you prepare for positive changes in the future.

Chapter 10
Putting It All Together

I f you picked up this book because you are 55 and hate your job, you now have some tools for making changes. If you are not 55 or do not hate your job, you can still use this guidance to better your career and your personal life. I hope this book has given you a lot of food for thought and action. Here is a look back at some key takeaways and recommended actions:

Chapter 1 Clarity:
Know the Destination Before You Chart the Course

If you don't know where you are going,
any road will get you there.

Lewis Carroll

Before you embark on any career journey, you need to become crystal clear on what your intentions are. Colleagues, partners, and other important people in your life may know you very well, but only you can decide what career moves are right for you.

Chapter 2: Workload:
Do You Really Hate It,
Or Do You Just Need to Do It Better?

Don't throw the baby out with the bathwater.

German Proverb

You may be overworked and frustrated. You may think you need to find a new job, but maybe what you really need is a new way to do your job. Maybe you need to realign the way responsibilities are shared among your team or automate what is done in your office. Take the time to reflect on the aspects of your job that need to change in order to turn the hate into love for your job.

Chapter 3 Attitude:
Are You Your Own Best Friend or Worst Foe?

There is nothing either good or bad,
but thinking makes it so.

William Shakespeare

Having a good attitude is something like having good health. It allows you to face everything else in your life with energy and optimism. Consider whether your attitude may be holding you back. If you have to admit that it is, you have taken the first step toward changing it.

Chapter 4: Financial Factors:
How Much Is Enough?

I finally know what distinguishes man
from the other beasts: financial worries.

Jules Renard

Do you feel chained to your job because you have heavy financial obligations? You don't see bumper stickers any more that say, "The one who dies with the most toys wins." Many people are unloading "stuff" to travel more lightly. That may be an option for you to consider while trying to regain your passion for your career.

Chapter 5: Philanthropy and Passion: Put Your Energy Where Your Heart Is

I truly believe that philanthropy and commerce can work together.

Donna Karan

Some people work at jobs that allow them to pursue their passions, but that is not the only way to fulfill your need to make a difference. You can work to support your family and use philanthropy or volunteerism as a way to give back to a cause that is meaningful to you. Giving back can give you a better feeling of balance in your life.

Chapter 6: Flexibility: Stretching Makes You Stronger

Have a plan, but be open to opportunity.

Ralph Raikes

Being flexible and stretching yourself physically and mentally will help you to achieve success, however you see it, and also enjoy the journey. Flexibility allows you to see more opportunities for growth, challenges, fun, and friendships to name just a few benefits.

Chapter 7: Awareness, Acknowledgement, and Appreciation: Creating an A Team

I can live for two months on a good compliment.

Mark Twain

Studies show that what workers want even more than a raise is appreciation. If you want to improve the atmosphere at work, strive to foster a culture of appreciation.

Chapter 8: Networking:
With Help from Your Friends

*If you want to go somewhere, it is best to find someone who has
already been there.*

Robert Kiyosaki

A strong network is one of the most important assets you can develop.
Networking may come more easily to an outgoing person, but how to
meet and support others can be learned. Asking for help when you
need it may be hard at first, but you may be surprised to find out who
might actually be willing and able to give you a hand on your journey.

Chapter 9: Coaching:
It Takes a Coach to Make a Champion

*All coaching is is taking a player
where he can't take himself.*

Bill McCartney

Years ago people struggled to do everything on their own, but now
the concept of being coached in everything from work to hobbies to
relationships is respected and, more often, expected.

I hope that the resources I have offered in this book will serve you
well in your career and in your life. Please visit www.rrgexec.com to
take advantage of other resources. Feel free to contact me personally
by phone or email for individual help.

Appendix

Being Held Financial Hostage

David L. Blaydes

B ob is 50 years old and hates his job. He would love to make a change but feels he's being held financial hostage. The sad part is that Bob put himself in this position.

Bob's parents had always urged him to be conscientious about his finances, telling him that the best way to be financially secure in the future was to create a financial plan early in life . . . but then life got busy. He had always waited for a more convenient time to establish a financial plan, yet a convenient time never came.

We're 20. We can't save money now. We're just getting started and don't earn very much. It takes everything we have to pay the bills and have some fun. Besides, we don't plan to retire for another 30 or 40 years. We have lots of time.

We're 30. Our family is growing. Our mortgage and car payments are very high. We need to invest in ourselves so we can get promoted. When we have higher-paying jobs, we will have money to invest. But we can't afford anything now.

We're 40. We spend all of our extra money on our children. We work hard and think we deserve a good lifestyle. We should be able to save after the children are on their own.

We're 50. Retirement is staring us in the face. We need to get started on our investments. But, our careers have peaked. We need all of our income to live. Our parents are facing healthcare issues that we may need to finance, and our children still need some help. We can't afford to set anything aside right now.

Bob is on course in five years to be saying:

We're 60. Who, us? Sure, investing is a great idea, but we're 65. Social Security doesn't go far. We should have started years ago, but it's too late now.

While the sooner the better, the truth is that it's never too late. Here are the three steps Bob should implement to start the process of becoming a freed hostage.

Step 1: Create a Personal Blueprint

Work with a qualified coach, such as Scott at Robinson Resource Group or another financial or life planner, to create a personal goals-based financial plan so that you can start living life based on design instead of default. The elements of the blueprint are:

Values: Certain things are important to you, but are you living those values day in, day out?

Meaningful Purpose: What are you "called" to do that will be remembered long after you're gone?

Compelling Vision: How can you achieve success and significance if you don't know what they look like?

Personal Mission: Once you know where you're trying to go, wouldn't it be easier to get there with a map?

Goals (specific, measurable, achievable, compatible): Wouldn't it be helpful to track your progress along the way?

Once the blueprint is completed or at least started, which can be done by either a coach or a financial advisor who uses such a process as the foundation of their financial planning, you need to find a qualified financial professional to assist you with your planning.

Step 2: Select a Financial Planner

Credentials: You want to work with an advisor that has financial planning credentials so that the advisor is more likely to be financial planning-based than just sales- and/or commission-based. The more notable credentials are:

- CFP™: Certified Financial Planner

- RFC: Registered Financial Consultant

- AIF: Accredited Investment Fiduciary

- MS: Masters in Financial Planning

History: In addition to credentials, you should also check the disciplinary history of the advisor. This can be accomplished by conducting a "broker check" with Financial Industry Regulatory Authority FINRA, the industry's regulatory agency (www.finra.org).

Area of Specialty: Just as you would go to a cardiologist instead of a dermatologist for heart-related issues, you should go to an advisor who specializes in your area of need. An advisor that specializes in working with individuals as they prepare for a job change or retirement is different from one who specializes in working with business owners.

Experience: Just as you would be hesitant to go to a doctor fresh out of med school, a financial advisor with a couple decades of experience is advisable.

Personal Comfort Level: While we're talking about doctors, "bedside manner" is important. You want to work with someone you're comfortable with so that you're more likely to return for annual reviews in order to keep your financial plan current.

Step 3: Establish a Financial Plan

Once personal goals are identified, a financial plan needs to be generated to allow the personal blueprint to become an affordable reality. Financial planning is accomplished through the following steps:

Gathering client data and determining goals and expectations. The financial planner asks about the client's financial situation, personal and financial goals, and attitude toward risk. The planner gathers all necessary documents before giving advice.

Analyzing and evaluating the client's financial status. The financial planner analyzes client information to assess his or her current situation and determine what must be done to achieve the client's goals. Depending on the services requested, this assessment could include analyzing the client's assets, liabilities, cash flow, current insurance coverage, investments, or tax strategies.

Developing and presenting the financial planning recommendations and/or alternatives. The financial planner offers financial planning recommendations that address the client's goals, based on the information the client provided. The planner reviews the recommendations with the client to allow the client to make informed decisions. The planner listens to client concerns and revises recommendations as appropriate.

Implementing the financial planning recommendations. The financial planner and client agree on how recommendations will be carried out. The planner may carry out the recommendations for the client or serve as a "coach," coordinating the process with the client and other professionals, such as attorneys or stockbrokers.

Step 4: Monitor and Update

The client and financial planner monitor the client's progress toward the goals. The planner and the client should periodically meet to review the situation and adjust recommendations as needed. This step is oftentimes overlooked but it is a critical one. Not only is it important for one to establish and implement a plan, but it is just as important to keep it current. This is oftentimes considered the fourth step of the financial planning process, but due to how often it's overlooked, I have made it a separate step in the process.

An example will demonstrate the difference a plan can make. Bob's largest investment asset was his 401(k), yet he had no idea how to invest it. He had a coworker who had a Masters in Finance, so Bob asked him how he had his 401(k) invested and did the same. His problem was that the coworker was 30 years younger and therefore was invested in a very aggressive fashion. As a result, Bob lost 50% of his 401(k) during the 2008-09 recession.

In reality, Bob did not need nor want the risk that was unknowingly associated with the investments he chose. A financial plan showed that Bob really only needed around a 6% rate of return. He could, therefore, use an asset allocation model designed for such a return with the intent to substantially reduce his risk.

The key here is that you have to determine what rate of return you need in order to accomplish your financial goals before you can determine the best asset allocation of your portfolio. And the only way to do that is to start with the plan, not the investment.

In summary, people don't plan to fail, they fail to plan. This can result in being held financial hostage to your current job. You may be one good coach and financial plan away from freedom.

Disclosure

1. *Opinions voiced in this chapter/Appendix are not intended to provide specific advice and should not be construed as recommendations for any individual. To determine which investments may be appropriate for you, consult with your financial, tax, or legal professional. Please remember that investment decisions should be based on an individual's goals, time horizon, and tolerance for risk. Furthermore, any listing of a vendor or product does not constitute an endorsement or warranty of the vendor or product by the National Planning Corporation (NPC). NPC is not to be held responsible for and may not be held liable for the adequacy of the information available. David Blaydes, Retirement Planners International, Inc. and NPC are separate and unrelated companies.*

2. *Asset allocation strategies are designed in an effort to optimize risk and reward, but cannot guarantee a profit or protect against a loss.*

3. *All examples used are for hypothetical illustration only, not indicative of any particular investment, actual results will vary.*

4. *Security and advisory services offered through National Planning Corporation (NPC), Member FINRA/SIPC, a Registered Investment Adviser. RPI, Inc. and NPC are separate and unrelated companies.*

Acknowledgements

The book is possible thanks to all of the clients with whom I have had the privilege to work. It is through their desire to obtain a higher level of leadership and their efforts to become a better mentor and boss to those they lead that this book was created.

In addition, all of us at Robinson Resource Group would like to thank our own coaches, mentors, and the people we have worked with us in our careers and have assisted us and guided us as leaders and coaches.

It is very appropriate that I specifically thank:

- My wife, Deb, without whose love and support none of this would be possible.

- My good friend and supporter, David Blaydes, who was there for me both emotionally and personally.

- My personal mentor early on in my career, Tim Covey, who always reminded me that "common sense prevails."

The professionals with whom I work, including my assistant, Lynn Patton, and book coach, Dianne Morr. Without their dedication and support of my vision and pursuits I could not have pulled this off.

And finally my two dogs Camo and Howard who, regardless of the day, meet me at the door with a smile, a wagging tail, and a desire to be petted. That always puts things into perspective.

About the Author

Scott Robinson is the founder of Robinson Resource Group, a premier, boutique firm specializing in senior level retained search and executive coaching. After 25 years of founding, growing, and leading the largest full service human resources firm in the Midwest and serving as a trusted advisor to executives in the C-suite and senior business leaders, Scott Robinson chose a transition of his own. He returned to his entrepreneurial roots to launch RRG.

Drawing on his 35 years experience in the human capital industry and his educational training—an MS in psychology as well as an MBA—Scott is uniquely prepared to guide this generation of senior leaders with transition, performance, and crisis coaching. He understands the new reality in the marketplace where personal growth and strategic thinking are more important than corporate seniority.

Scott is certified by the Worldwide Association of Business Coaches as a Registered Corporate Coach™—one of fewer than 1000 such certified coaches worldwide. He is a member of the Institute of Coaching Professional Association at McLean Hospital—a Harvard Medical School affiliate. He currently serves as the president of the Crohn's & Colitis Foundation of America.

Contact Scott Robinson

Scott extends a warm invitation to email him at scott@rrgexec.com or call 708-888-1RRG to:

- Comment on this book and share your thoughts
- Order additional copies of *I'm 55 and I Hate My Job*
- Discuss consulting or coaching
- Book Scott to speak for your company or association